Get ready for

KINDERGARTEN

Letters • Numbers • Colors • Shapes
Sizes • Opposites • Logic • Counting

Little
GENIUS
Books

This book belongs to:

Draw a portrait of yourself.

Letter A

Practice writing the letter A, then write the words below.

Circle every letter A in this word mishmash.
Draw an X on the word that doesn't contain the letter A.

BASKETBALL

BADMINTON

BALL   skates

KARATE   KAYAK

RACKET

PALM

VOLLEYBALL

SOCCER   PADDLE

BASEBALL

Letter B

Practice writing the letter B, then write the words below. Connect each word to the matching picture.

B b B b

BELL

ball

BANANA

boat

BIRD

Circle every letter B in this word mishmash.

LIBRARY

TABLE

HOBBY

BICYCLE

BABY

BANANA

BOOK

BASKETBALL

BUTTERFLY

Connect the images with names that start with a "b" sound to the letter B.

Letter C

Practice writing the letter C, then write the words below. Connect each word to the matching picture.

C c C c

CRAYON

cake

CAT

clock

CACTUS

Circle the images with a name that starts with the letter C.

Practice writing the letter D, then write the words below. Connect each word to the matching picture.

D D d D d

DOG

domino

DRAWING

dancer

DOLL

Letter E

Practice writing the letter E, then write the words below.

E e E e

elephant

ELF

envelope

EGG

elbow

Letter F

Practice writing the letter F, then write the words below. Connect each word to the matching picture.

F f F f

FLAG

fish

FLOWER

flamingo

FROG

Write the letter F to complete the words.

___ e n c e

j e l l y ___ i s h

___ o r k

g i r a ___ e

___ o o t b a l l

___ o x

c o ___ e e

___ l o u r

Letter G

Practice writing the letter G, then write the words below. Connect each word to the matching picture.

G g G g

GIRAFFE

gloves

GIFT

guitar

GHOST

Help the baby giraffe find its way through the maze.

Letter H

Practice writing the letter H, then write the words below. Connect each word to the matching picture.

H h H h

HEART

hand

HAMMER

harp

HORSE

Practice writing the letter I, then write the words below.

I i I i

IGUANA

idea

Find the 7 differences between the two pictures.

Circle the pictures with names that end with an "I" sound.

Help the small i find the capital I.

i →

↓

I

Letter J

Practice writing the letter J, then write the words below. Connect each word to the matching picture.

J j J j

JAGUAR

juice

JET

jam

JACKET

Draw your favorite toy.

Letter K

Practice writing the letter K, then write the words below. Connect each word to the matching picture.

K k K k

KOALA

kiwi

KART

kayak

KIMONO

Trace and circle all the letter Ks.

Letter L

Practice writing the letter L, then write the words below. Connect each word to the matching picture.

L l L l

LETTUCE

lion

LAMP

lizard

LADYBUG

Draw a line from each object to the correct word.

lemon   lighthouse

lock   lollipop

leaf   lamb

lips   ladder

Letter M

Practice writing the letter M, then write the words below. Connect each word to the matching picture.

M m M m

MONKEY

mountain

MOON

mermaid

MIRROR

Practice writing the word MONSTER.

Monster

Draw the scariest monster you can think of.

Letter N

Practice writing the letter N, then write the words below. Connect each word to the matching picture.

N n N n

NEST

nine

NINJA

notes

NET

Circle all the letter Ns.

A m n h H N f

N a E M n C V

t N q T W m D

M F u n O z N

n G I w N b M

S N B m R H n

t N q T N m D

n G I w n b M

a m n W H N f

Practice writing the letter O, then write the words below.

O o O o

octopus

OWL

Circle all the words that end with the "o" sound.

DOG PIANO JUDO

BOAT TUBA RADIO

BANJO RADIO KARATE

HAT TOMATO

Letter P

Practice writing the letter P, then write the words below. Connect each word to the matching picture.

P p P p

PLANT

pumpkin

PAINT

penguin

PLANET

Practice writing the word PLANET. Color the drawing.

Planet

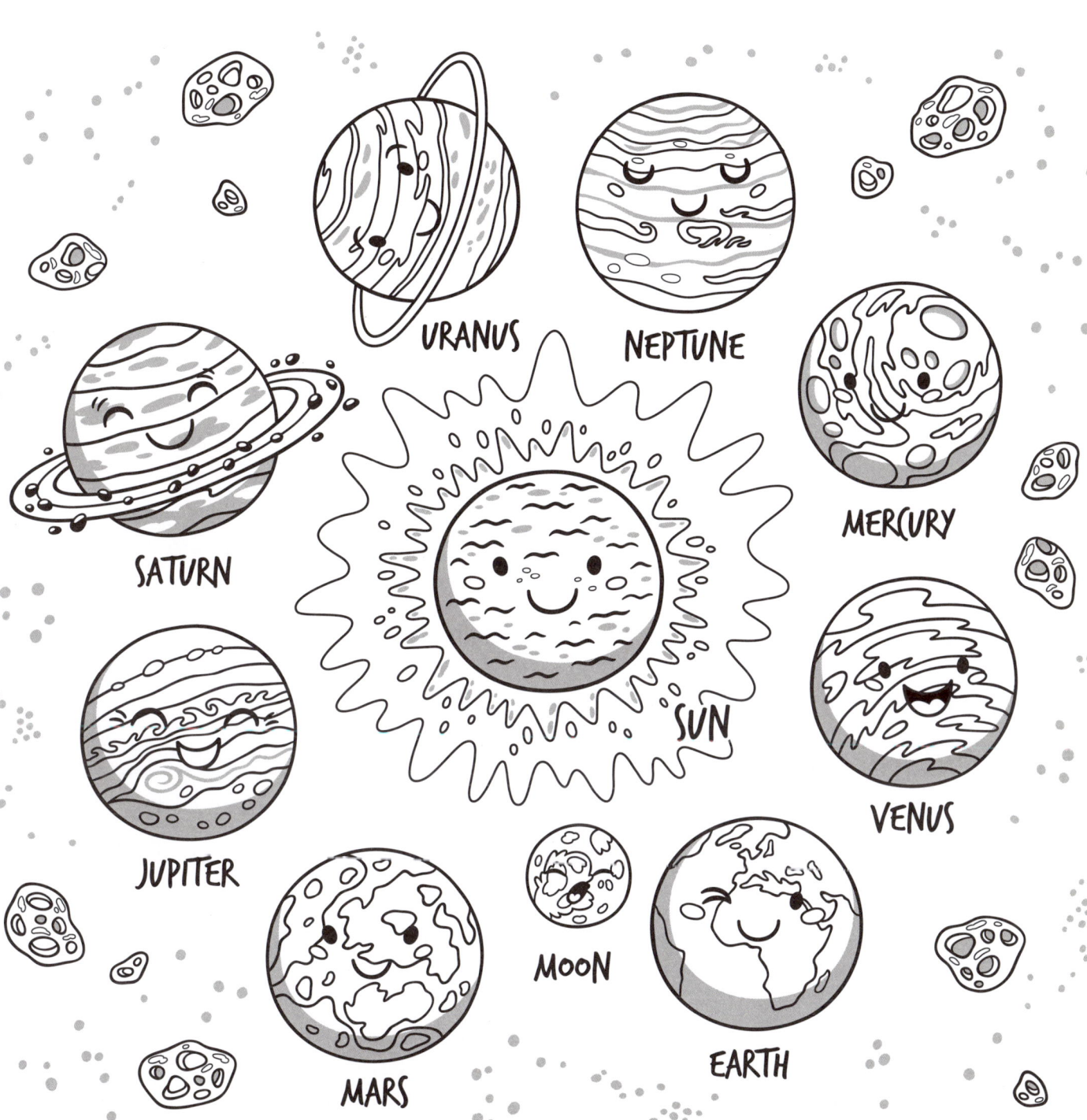

URANUS

NEPTUNE

MERCURY

SATURN

SUN

JUPITER

VENUS

MARS

MOON

EARTH

Letter Q

Practice writing the letter Q, then write the words below. Connect each word to the matching picture.

Q q Q q

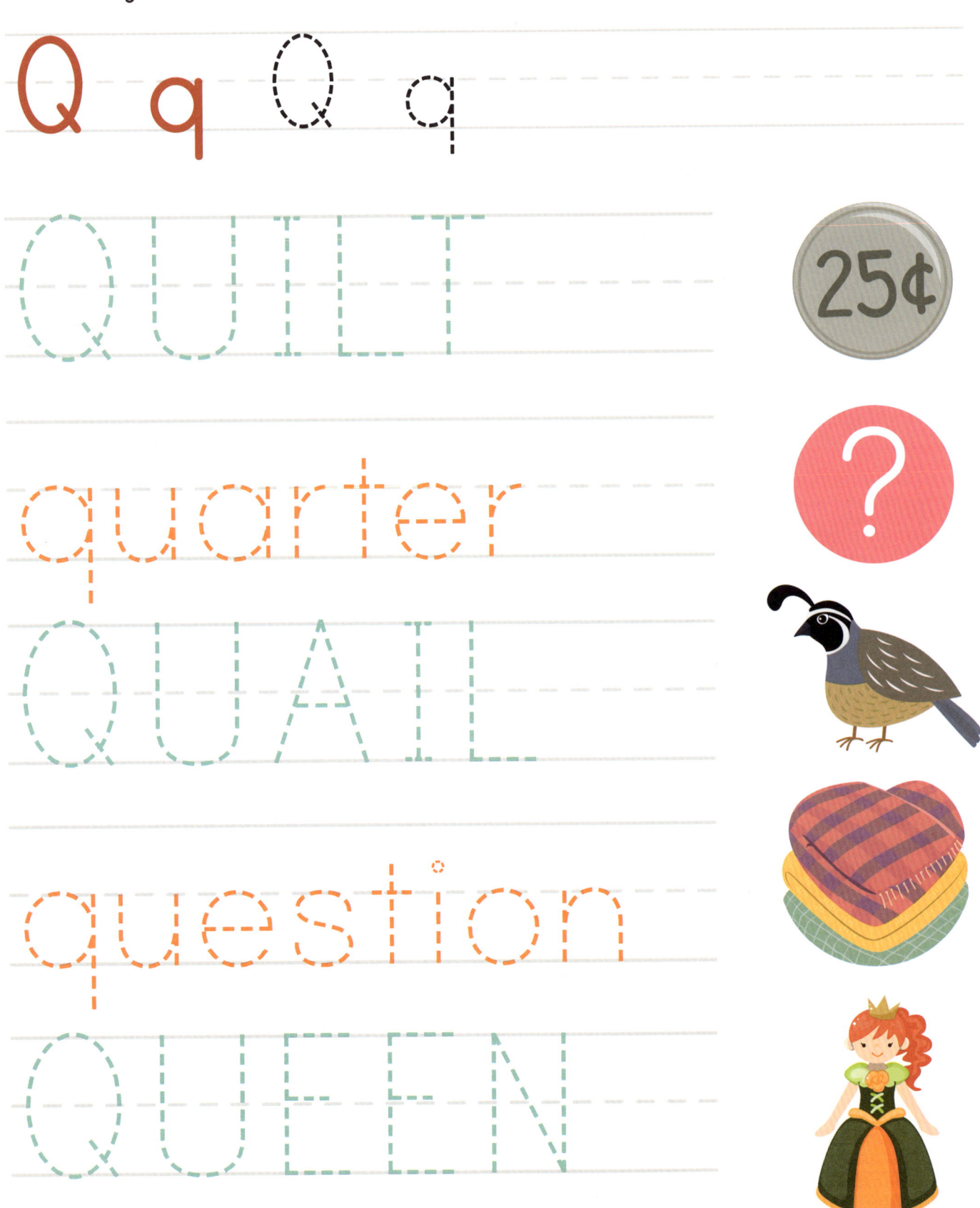

QUILT

quarter

QUAIL

question

QUEEN

Practice writing the word AQUARIUM. Draw all kinds of creatures inside the aquarium.

Aquarium

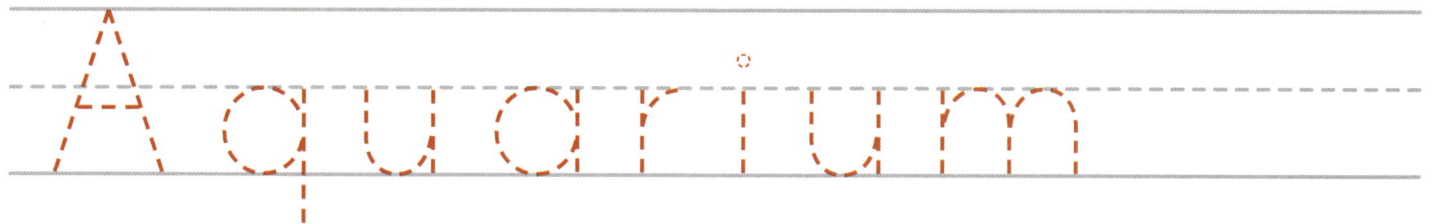

Letter R

Practice writing the letter R, then write the words below. Connect each word to the matching picture.

R r R r

RULER

rainbow

RADISH

rose

RAIN

Color the letters that form the word RATTLESNAKE.

Practice writing the letter S, then write the words below. Connect each word to the matching picture.

S s S s

SNAIL

snake

SUN

spaceship

SOCKS

Circle every S in this word mishmash.

SPIDER

SHIP

STEP

STUDENT

SEAHORSE

INSIDE

SLICE

Circle the letters that form the word GRASSHOPPER.

Letter T

Practice writing the letter T, then write the words below. Connect each word to the matching picture.

T t T t

TURTLE

tractor

TIGER

table

TENT

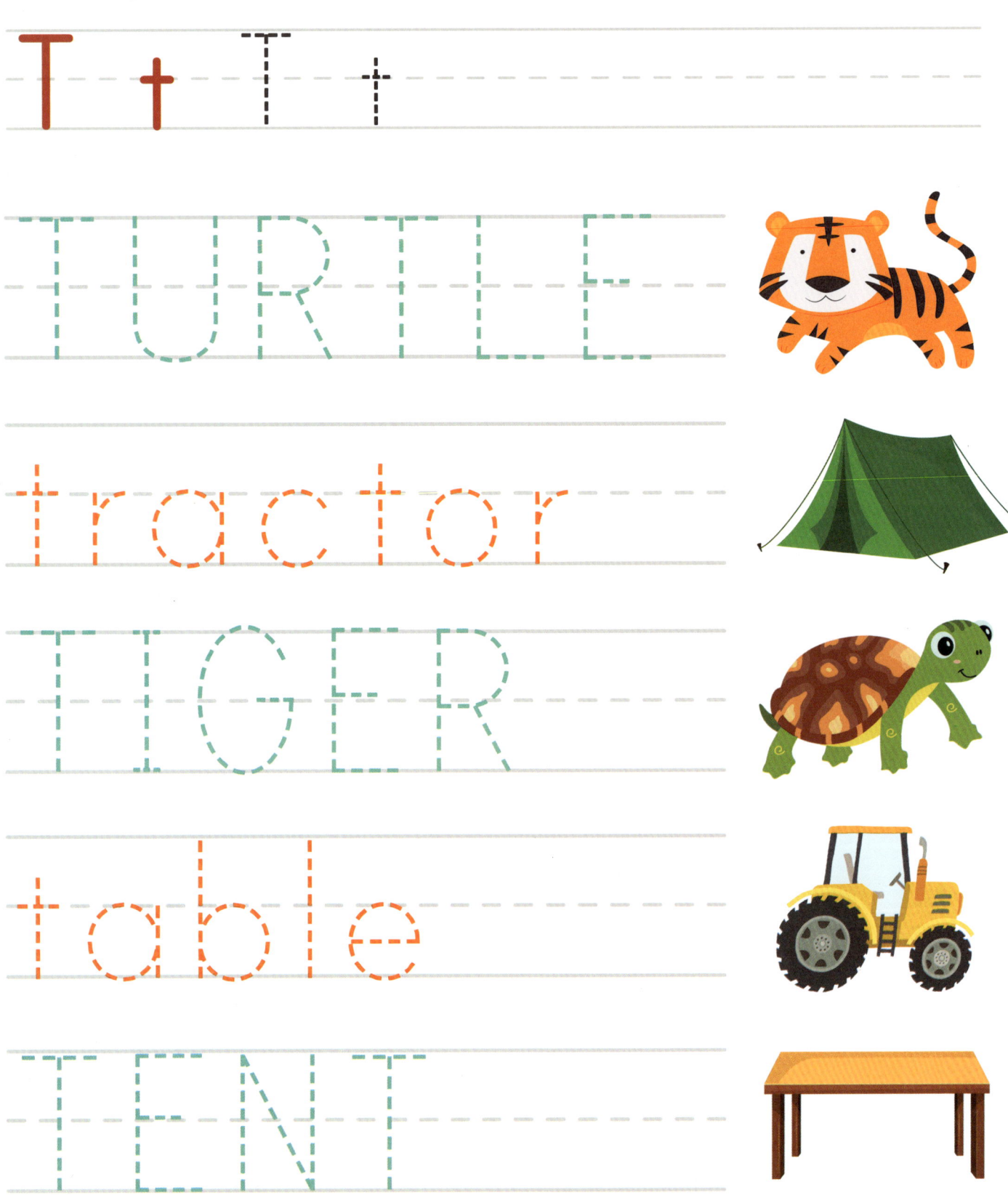

Help Thomas the turtle find his friend Tobby.

Letter U

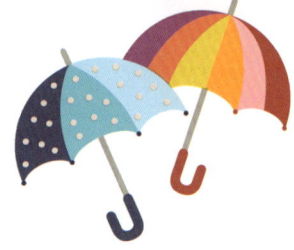

Practice writing the letter U, then write the words below.

U u U u

UNICORN

umbrella

Color the unicorn.

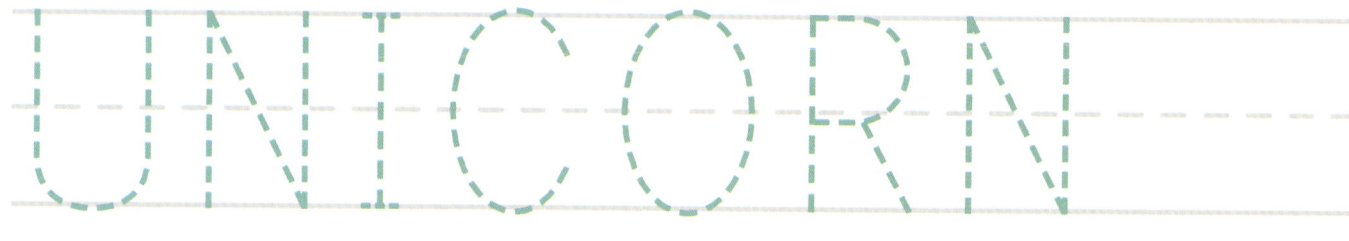

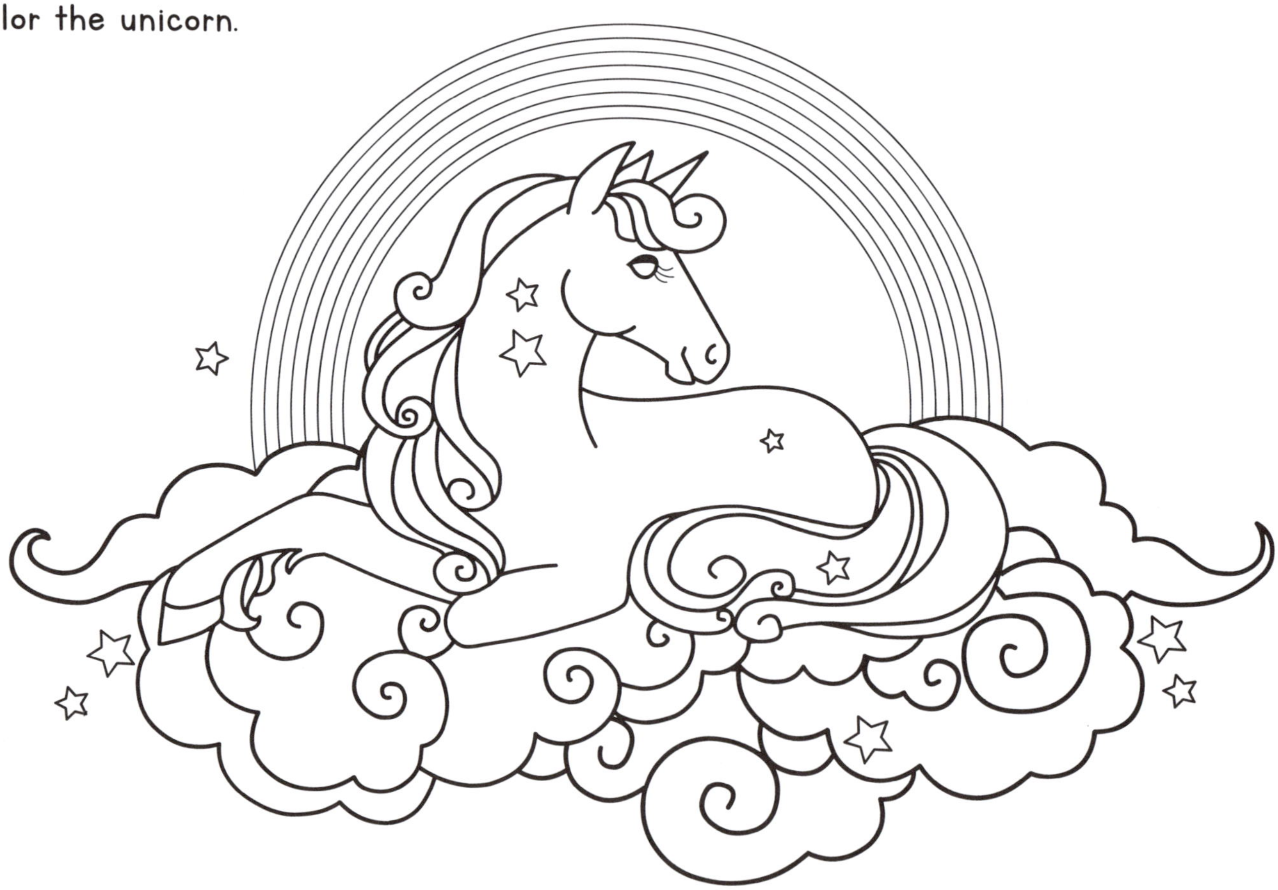

Write the missing vowels
by following the secret code.

A E I O U

_ L _ V _

R _ D _ N G MY

B _ CYCL _ D _ WN

TH _ STR _ _ T.

Letter V

Practice writing the letter V, then write the words below. Connect each word to the matching picture.

V v v v

VIOLIN

volleyball

VASE

vampire

VACUUM

Write in the missing letters by following the secret code.

_ O _ O _ _ Y _ _ E

_ _ A I _

_ A _

_ I K E

_ _ U _ K

S A I _ _ O A _

A _ _ U _ A _ _ E

_ _ A _ _ O _

Letter W

Practice writing the letter W, then write the words below. Connect each word to the matching picture.

W   w   W   w

WAGON

wapiti

KIWI

Circle the words that have the letter W.

VOTE

PLOW

CROW

ZEBRA

CAVE

WINDOW

WATER

Letter X

Practice writing the letter X, then write the words below. Connect each word to the matching picture.

X x X x

BOX

xylophone

SIX

saxophone

FOX

Draw a line from each word on the left to its plural form on the right.

TOOTH   ○   ○   MEN

WOMAN   ○   ○   MICE

FOOT   ○   ○   FEET

MAN   ○   ○   WOMEN

MOUSE   ○   ○   TEETH

Letter Y

Practice writing the letter Y, then write the words below. Connect each word to the matching picture.

Y y Y y

YO-YO

yogurt

YAK

coyote

YARN

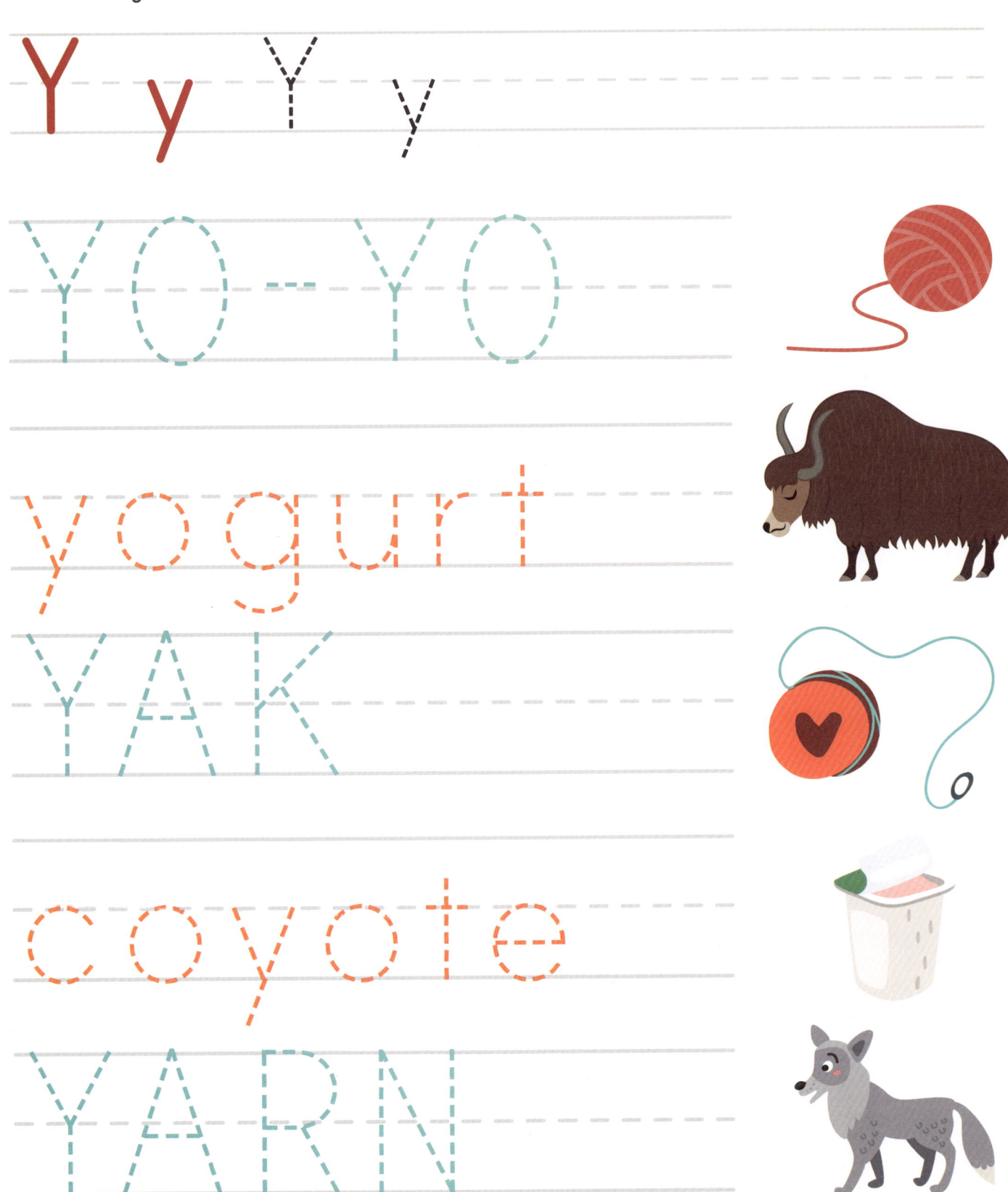

Practice writing the letter Z, then write the words below. Connect each word to the matching picture.

Z z Z z

ZEBRA

zero

ZIGZAG

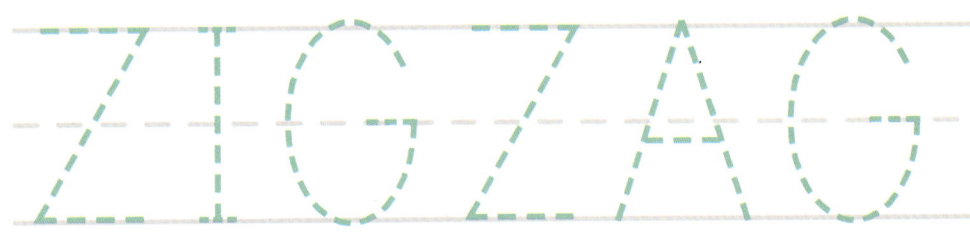

Trace the dotted lines.

Find and circle the 4 misspelled words.

ZEBRA ZEBRA zebra ZEBRA

zebra zibra ZEBRA zebra

ZEBRA ZEBRA zebra ZEBRA

zebra ZEBRA ZEBRA zobra

ZEBRA zebra zebra ZEBRA

zebra ZEPRA ZEBRA zebra

ZEBRA ZEBRA zebra ZEBRA

zebra ZEBRA zebra zebro

ZEBRA zebra ZEBRA ZEBRA

Draw a line from each animal to its name.

zebra

lion

elephant

crocodile

hippopotamus

ostrich

tiger

koala

Count 1, 2, 3, 4

Practice writing the numbers 1 to 4.

1 1 1

2 2 2

3 3 3

4 4 4

Count the items in each circle, and write your answer in the bubbles.

Circle the three products that are not made of dairy.

Count 5, 6, 7, 8

Practice writing the numbers 5 to 8.

5   5   5

6   6   6

7   7   7

8   8   8

Count the items in each circle and write your answer in the bubbles.

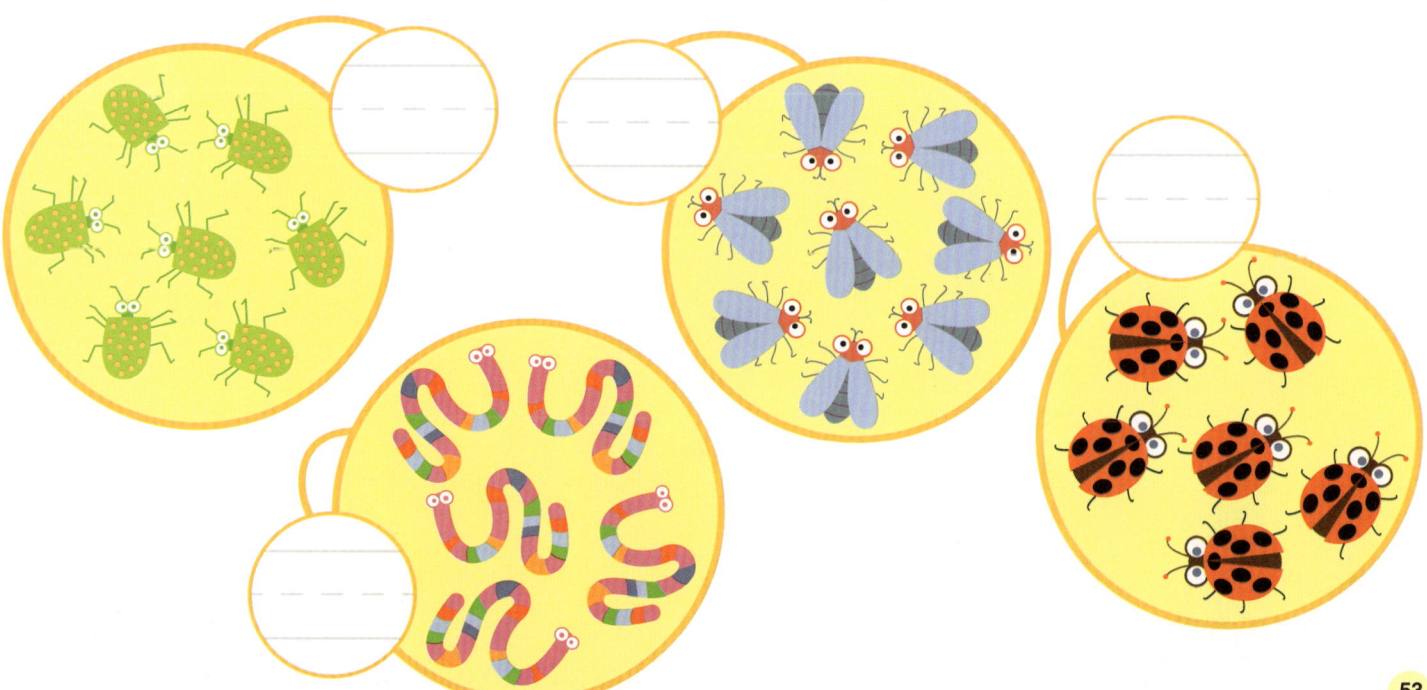

Count the birds that are inside of the cages and the ones that are outside of the cages, then write your answers in the bubbles.

Inside:

Outside:

Find the way through this maze by following the pattern.

Count the items in these equations and write your answer in the squares.

Write the numbers 1 to 4 in the bubbles, from the smallest dinosaur to the biggest.

Draw 5 yellow fish, 6 orange fish, 7 blue fish and 8 red fish.

Count 9, 10, 11, 12

Practice writing the numbers 9 to 12.

9   9   9

10   10   10

11   11   11

12   12   12

Circle 7 shovels, 8 vegetables and 9 flowers.

Count the items in each rectangle and circle the correct answer.

$$+ \quad = \quad 4 \quad 5 \quad 6$$

$$+ \quad = \quad 7 \quad 8 \quad 9$$

$$+ \quad = \quad 10 \quad 11 \quad 12$$

Solve these equations.

$$7 + 1 = \boxed{}$$

$$3 + 1 = \boxed{}$$

$$5 + 2 = \boxed{}$$

$$2 + 4 = \boxed{}$$

Count the number of fruit in each square and write your answer.

Count 13, 14, 15, 16

Practice writing the numbers 13 to 16.

13   13   13

14   14   14

15   15   15

16   16   16

Find the 13 differences between the two pictures.

Circle the following objects:

8 hats
6 pairs of gloves
14 shoes and boots

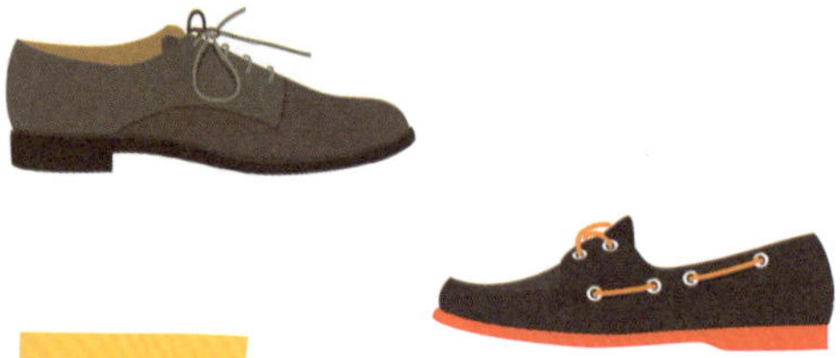

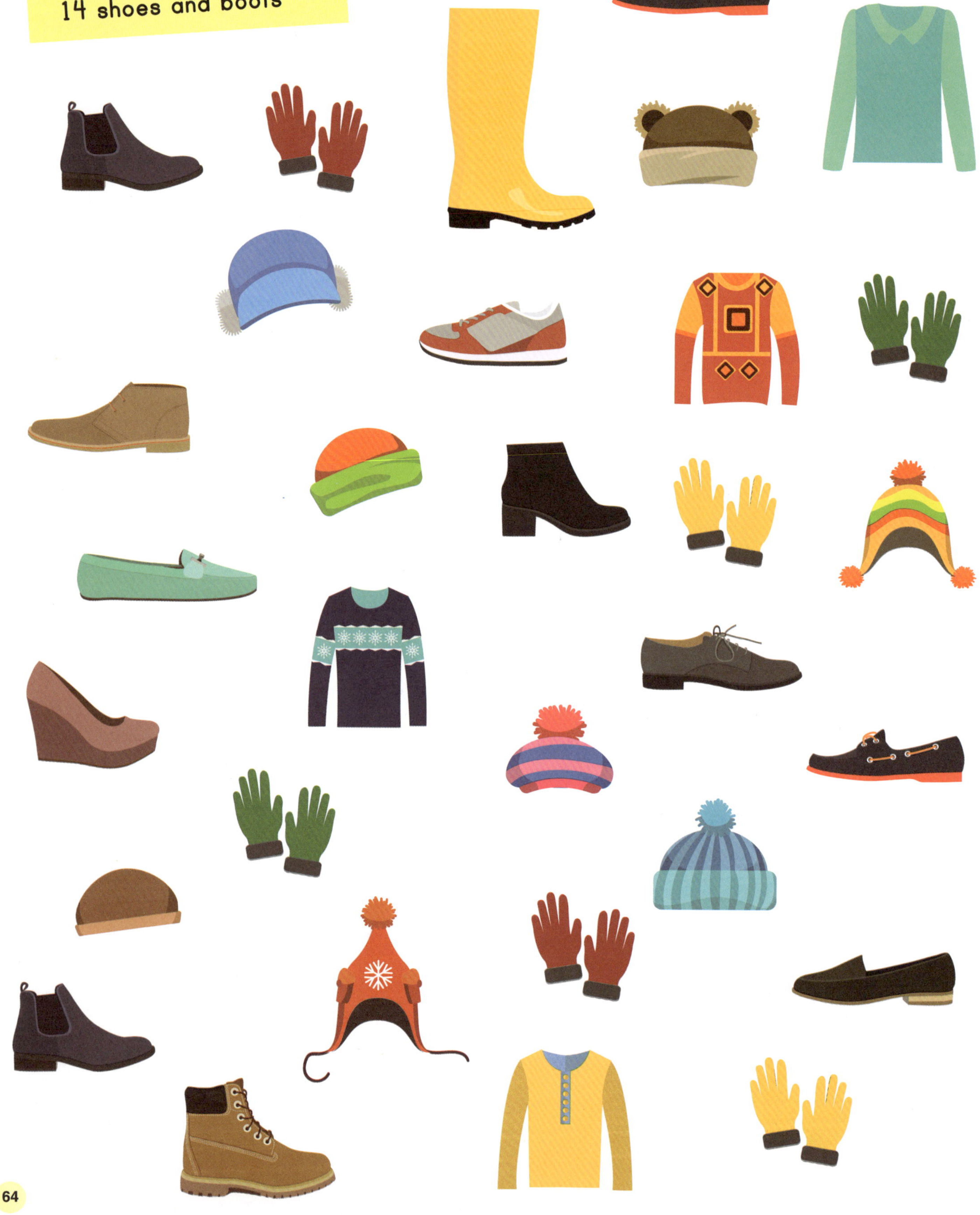

Count the different animals. Then fill in the correct grid square for each of the animals.

	1	2	3	4	5	6	7	8	9	10

Count 17, 18, 19, 20

Practice writing the numbers 17 to 20.

17   17   17

18   18   18

19   19   19

20   20   20

Circle the animals that have fur.

Count the number of dots and trace the answer.

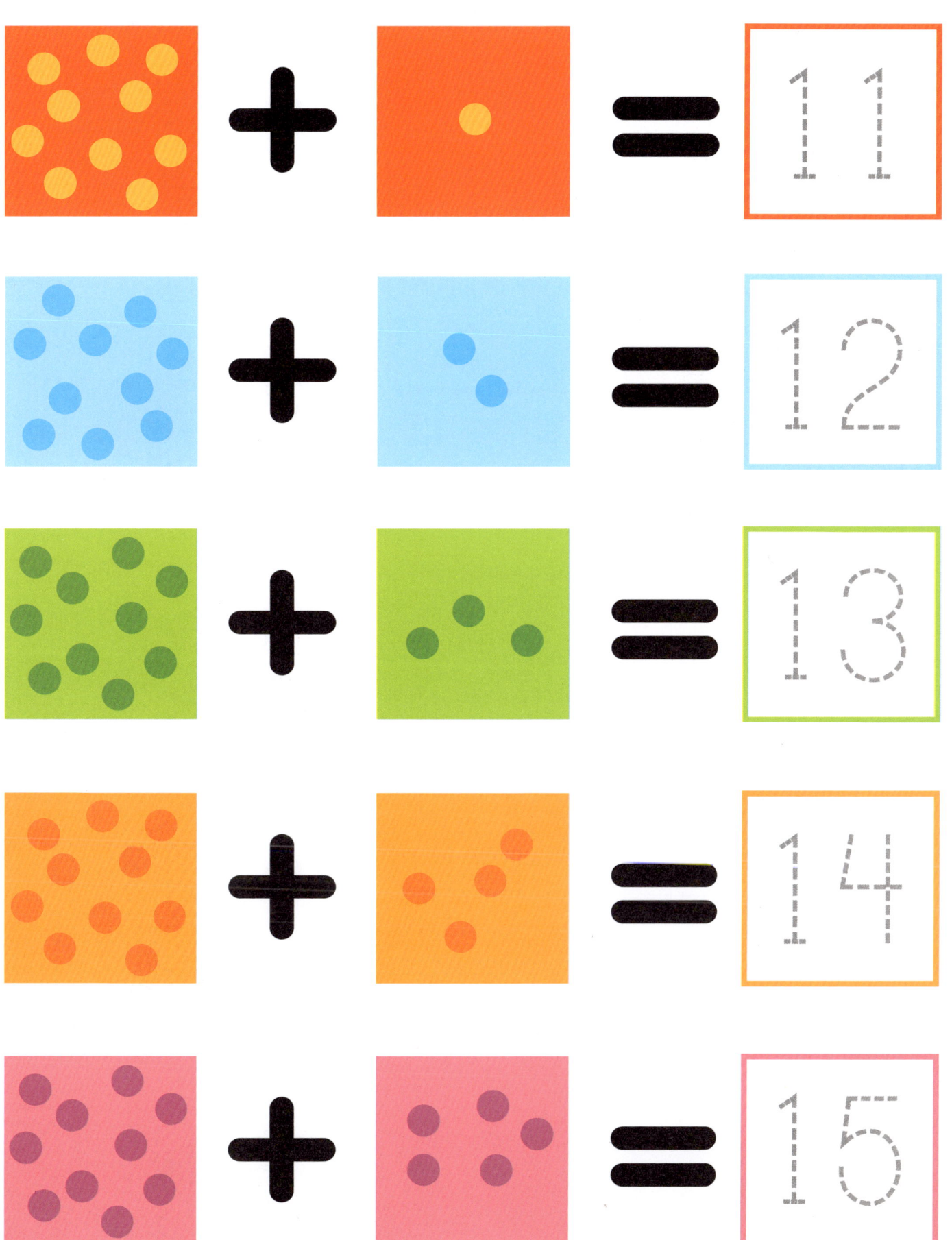

Connect each pair of sneakers to the correct box size.

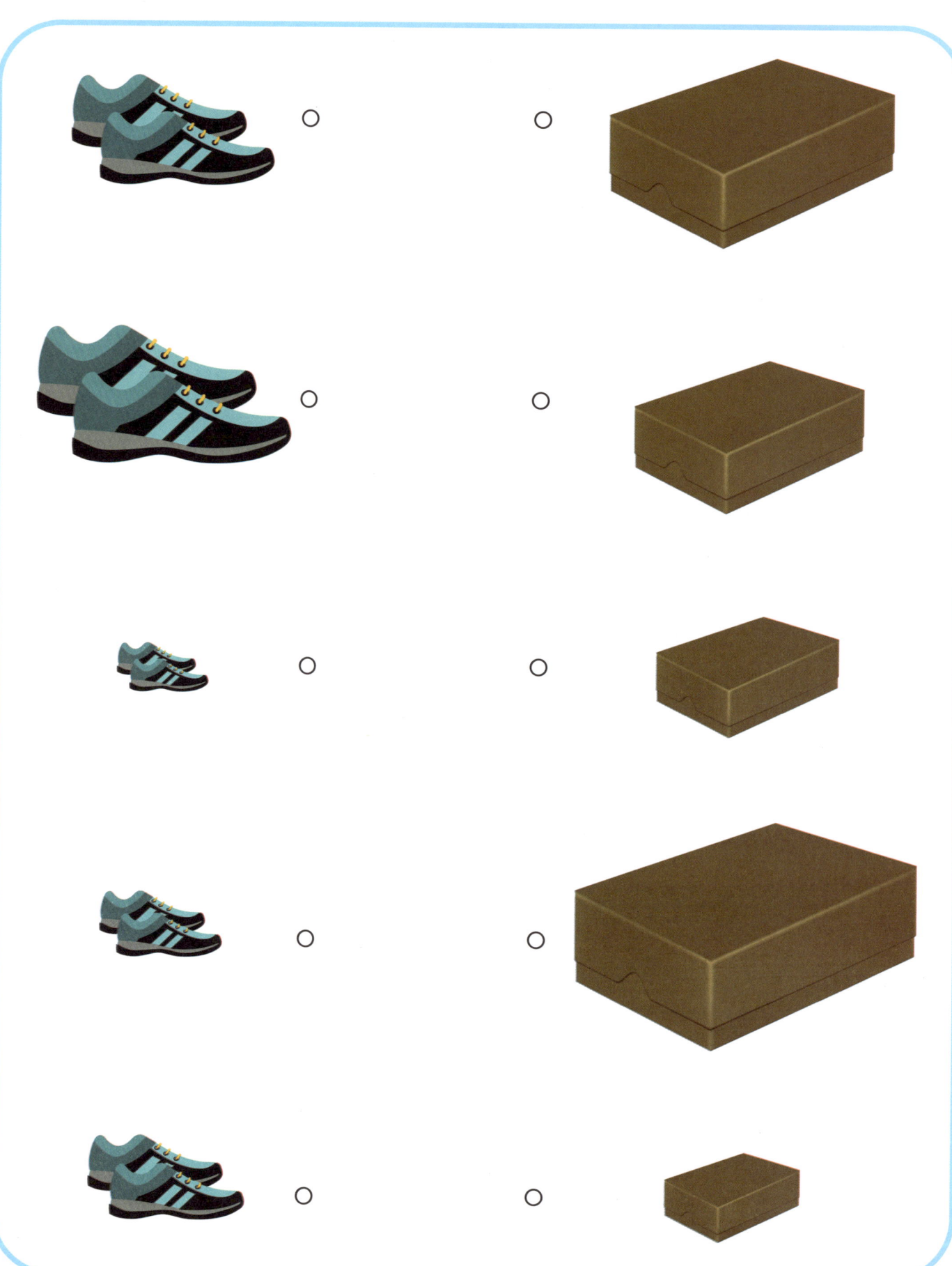

Count the number of dots and trace the answer.

Connect the numbers 1 to 20 and color the drawing.

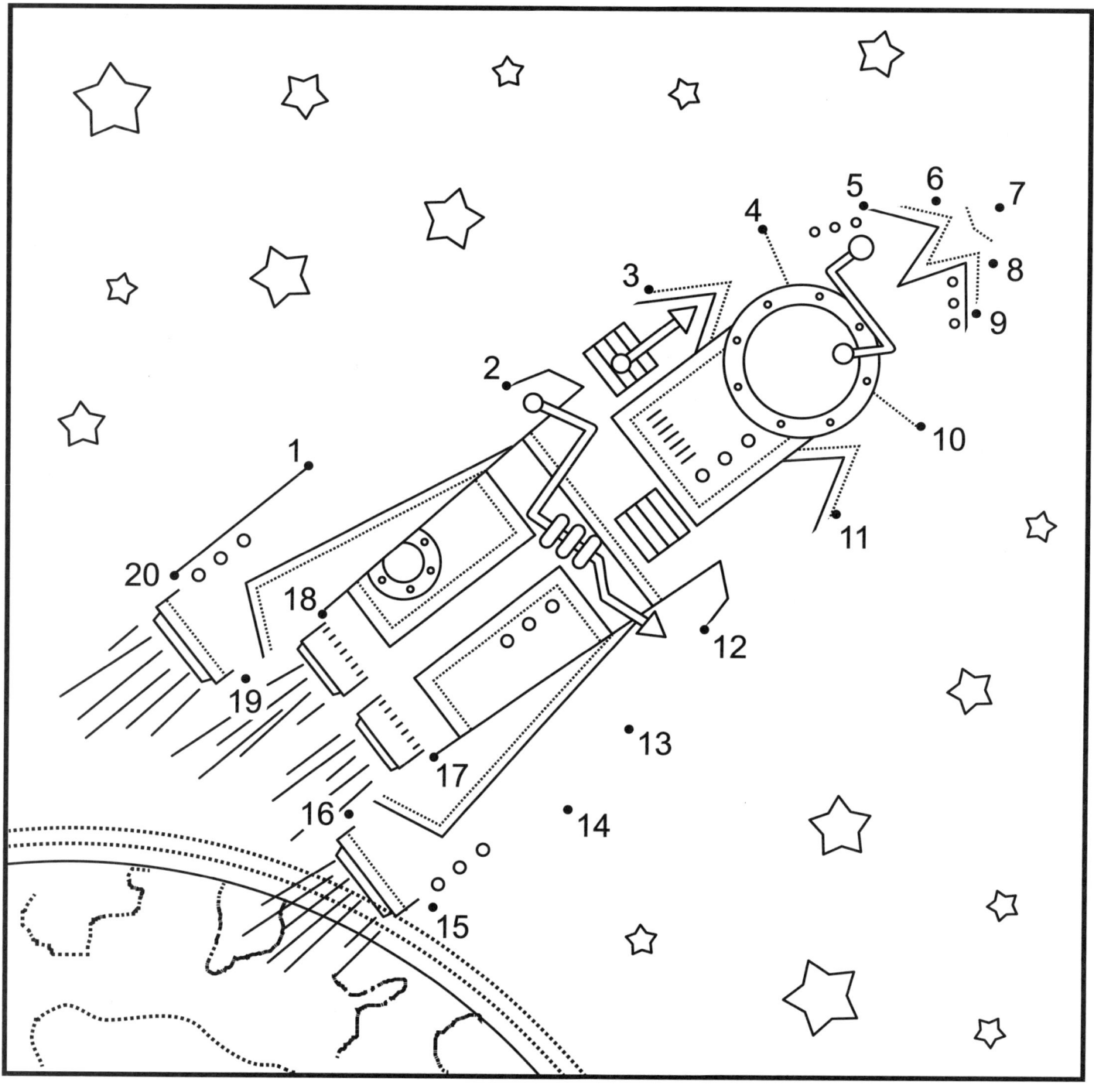

Count the number of hearts in the boxes on the left and draw an equal number of squares in the boxes on the right.

Count the number of flowers of each kind and write your answer in the circles below.

Count the items in each box and circle your answer.

= 8 9 10

= 11 12 13

= 6 7 8

Help the owl reach the forest by finding its way through the number maze.
Start on the number 1 and find your way to number 9. You have to travel in number
order and can only land on each number once.

		6	5	6	8	4
		3	4	7	5	3
2	1	2	5	6	3	6
3	7	5	6	1	8	7
4	6	1	7	8	9	6
6	5	6	8	7		
3	1	7	8	9		

Write numbers 1 to 20.

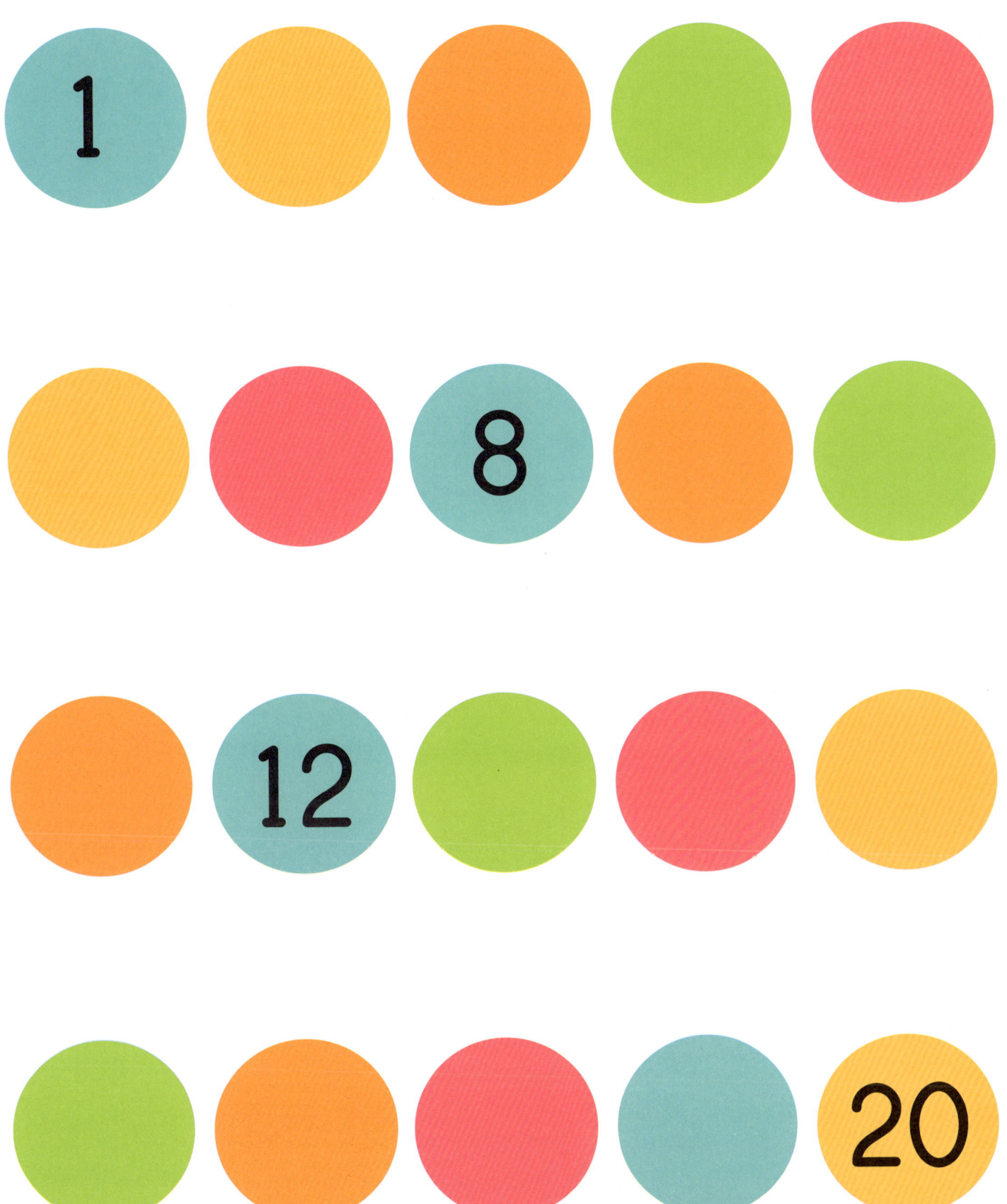

Square

Trace the squares using the same colors as the dotted lines.

Draw square windows for the school. Use the example in the corner if you need help.

Color 1 ice cream scoop ORANGE and 2 GREEN.

Triangle

Trace and color the flags.

Diamond

Complete each sequence with the correct shapes.

Rectangle

Color the rectangles in purple and the squares in orange.

Circle the following objects:

- 6 fire trucks
- 5 planes
- 7 police cars

82

Follow the sequence to find your way through the maze.

Find the 6 differences between the two pictures.

Left or right?
Circle in GREEN the vehicles heading towards the RIGHT. (⟶)
Circle in RED the vehicles heading towards the LEFT. (⟵)

Follow the instructions in the box to color the rocket ships.

- Color the rocket ship heading up in **BLUE**.
- Color the rocket ship heading left in **RED**.
- Color the rocket ship heading right in **GREEN**.

Connect each item to the correct bubble.

small

medium

large

Follow the sequence to find your way through the maze.

Trace the dotted lines.

Draw waves over and under the fish.

Each truck carries 4 cars: 2 at the bottom and 2 on the top.
Make groups of 4 cars and connect them to a truck.
How many cars are left?

Color the insects ORANGE.
Color the mushrooms BROWN.
Color the flowers YELLOW.
Color the cat any color you want.

Count the animals standing in front of the fence and the ones standing behind the fence. Write how many there are in the circles.

In front

Behind

Solve the equations, then use the color code to color in the butterfly.

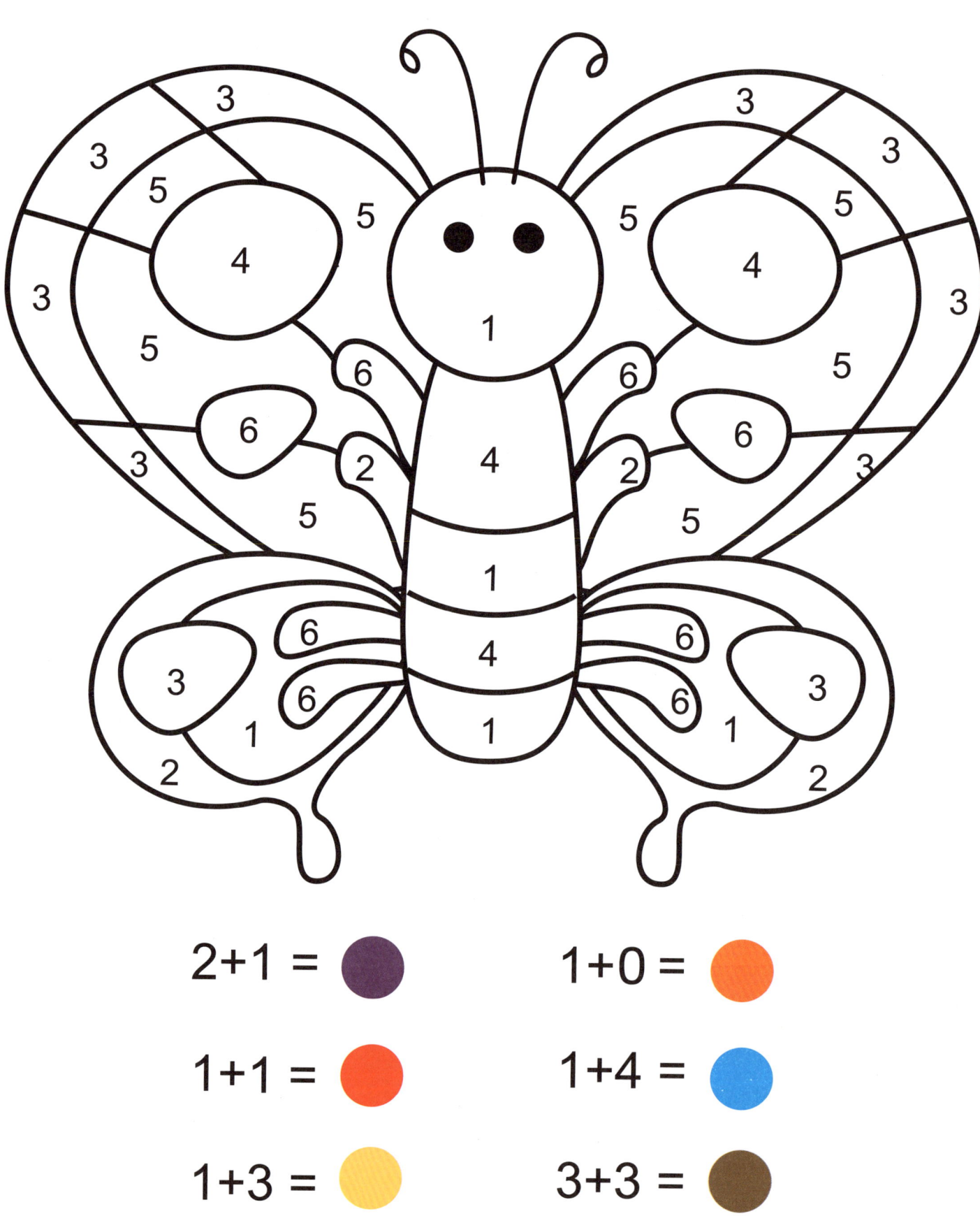

2+1 = ⬤ (purple)   1+0 = ⬤ (orange)

1+1 = ⬤ (red)   1+4 = ⬤ (blue)

1+3 = ⬤ (yellow)   3+3 = ⬤ (brown)

Circle the animals that live on a farm.

Which items below are green? Color them GREEN!

Draw a line from each animal to where it lives.

Color the second ball **RED**. Color the last ball **BLUE**.

Color the first racket **YELLOW**.

Color the two balls that are the same **RED**.

Circle the following sports items.

- 1 bicycle
- 2 red rackets
- 4 tennis balls

Trace the balls and color them in.

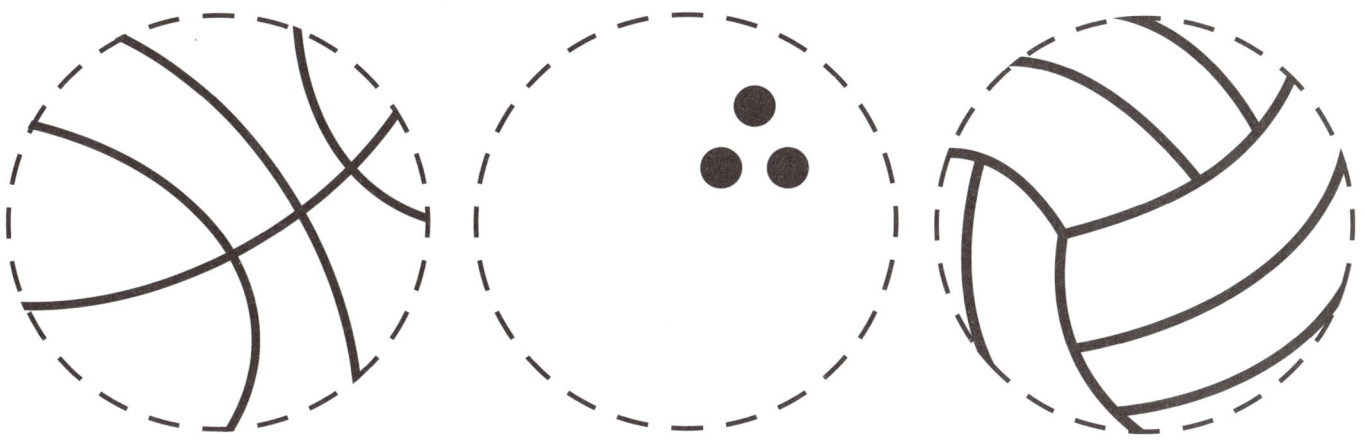

Circle the 4 items that are not round.

Draw a line from each cow to its shadow.

Read these words and write each word next to the correct number.

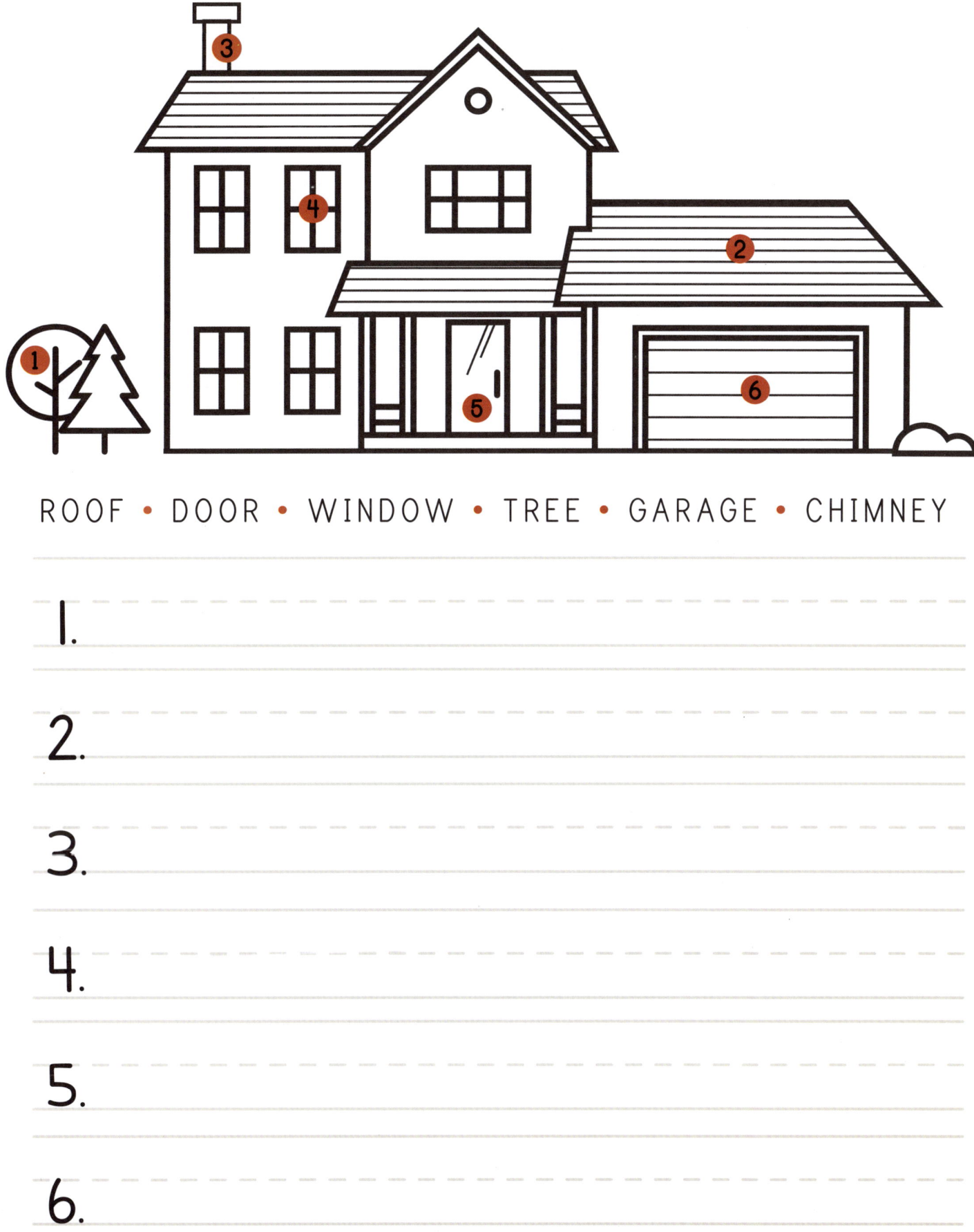

ROOF • DOOR • WINDOW • TREE • GARAGE • CHIMNEY

1.

2.

3.

4.

5.

6.

Can you name all the members of a family?

brother • sister • father
mother • grandfather • grandmother

Write the missing letters to complete the words.

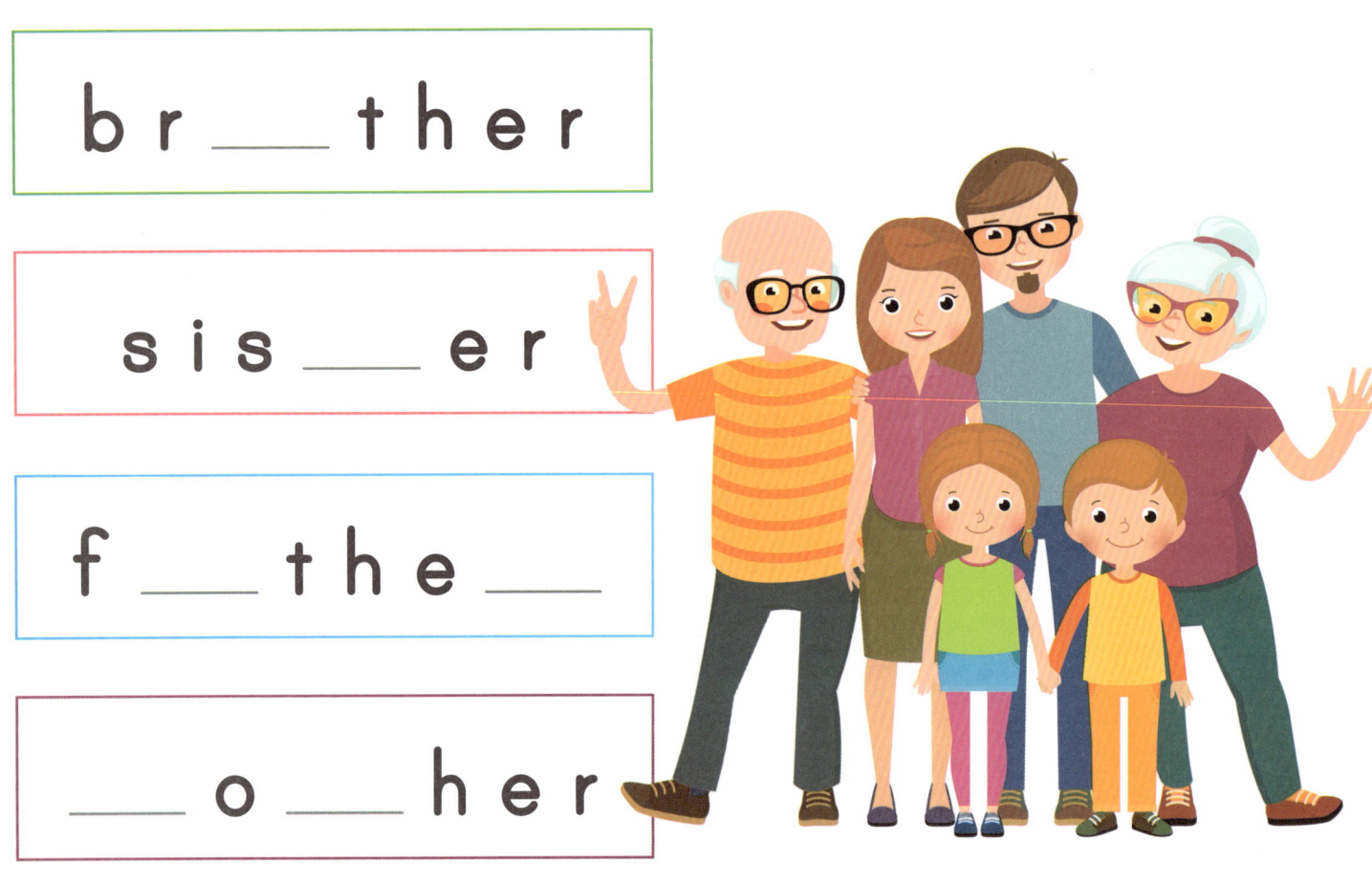

br ___ ther

sis ___ er

f ___ the ___

___ o ___ her

gran ___ ___ ather

gr ___ ndm ___ ther

Practice writing these words.

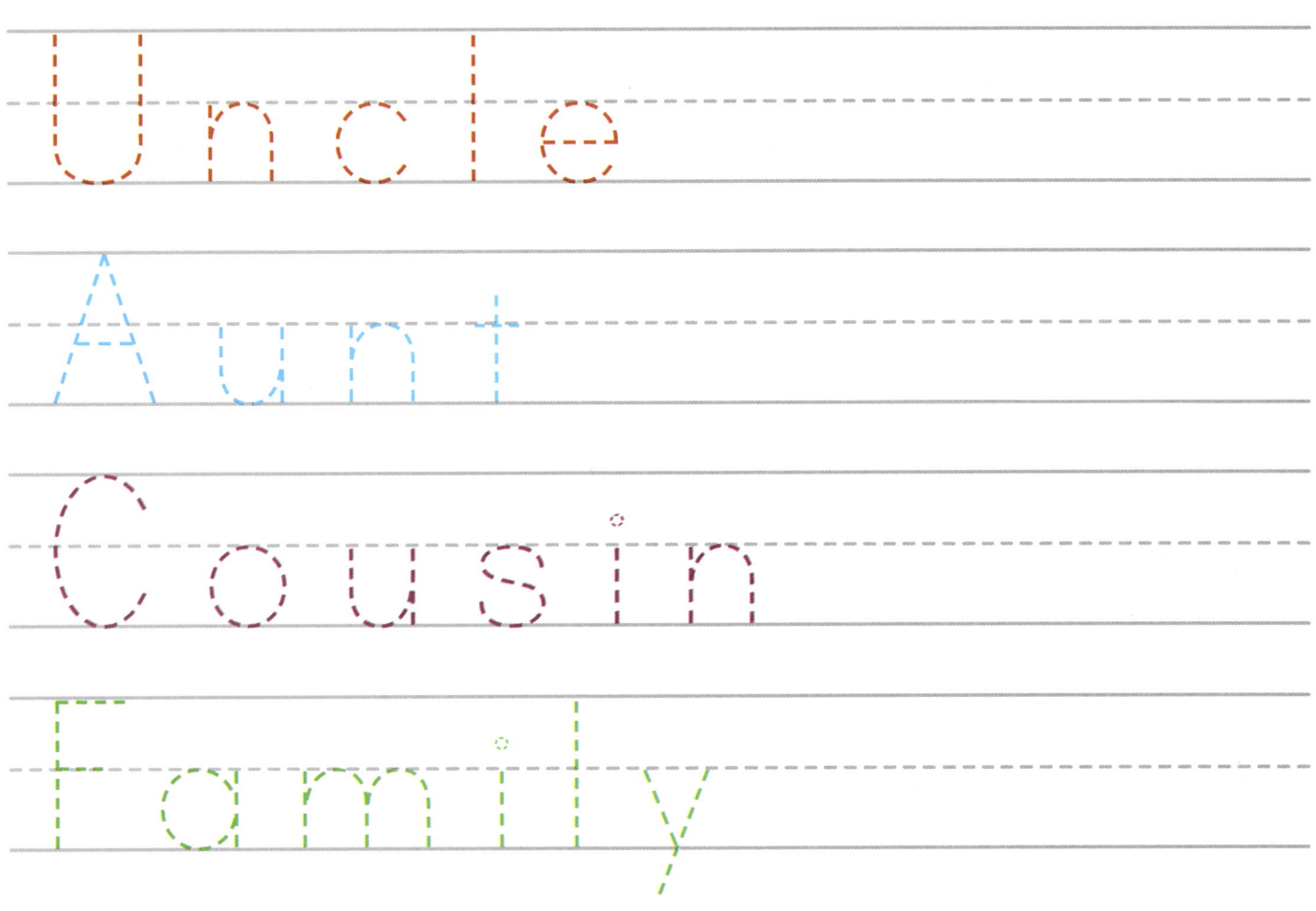

Uncle

Aunt

Cousin

Family

Answer the following questions. You can ask an adult to help you.

1 How many uncles do you have? _____

2 How many aunts do you have? _____

3 Do you have any cousins? YES   NO

4 How many cousins do you have?

Do you know these tropical fruits? Draw a line from each fruit to its name.

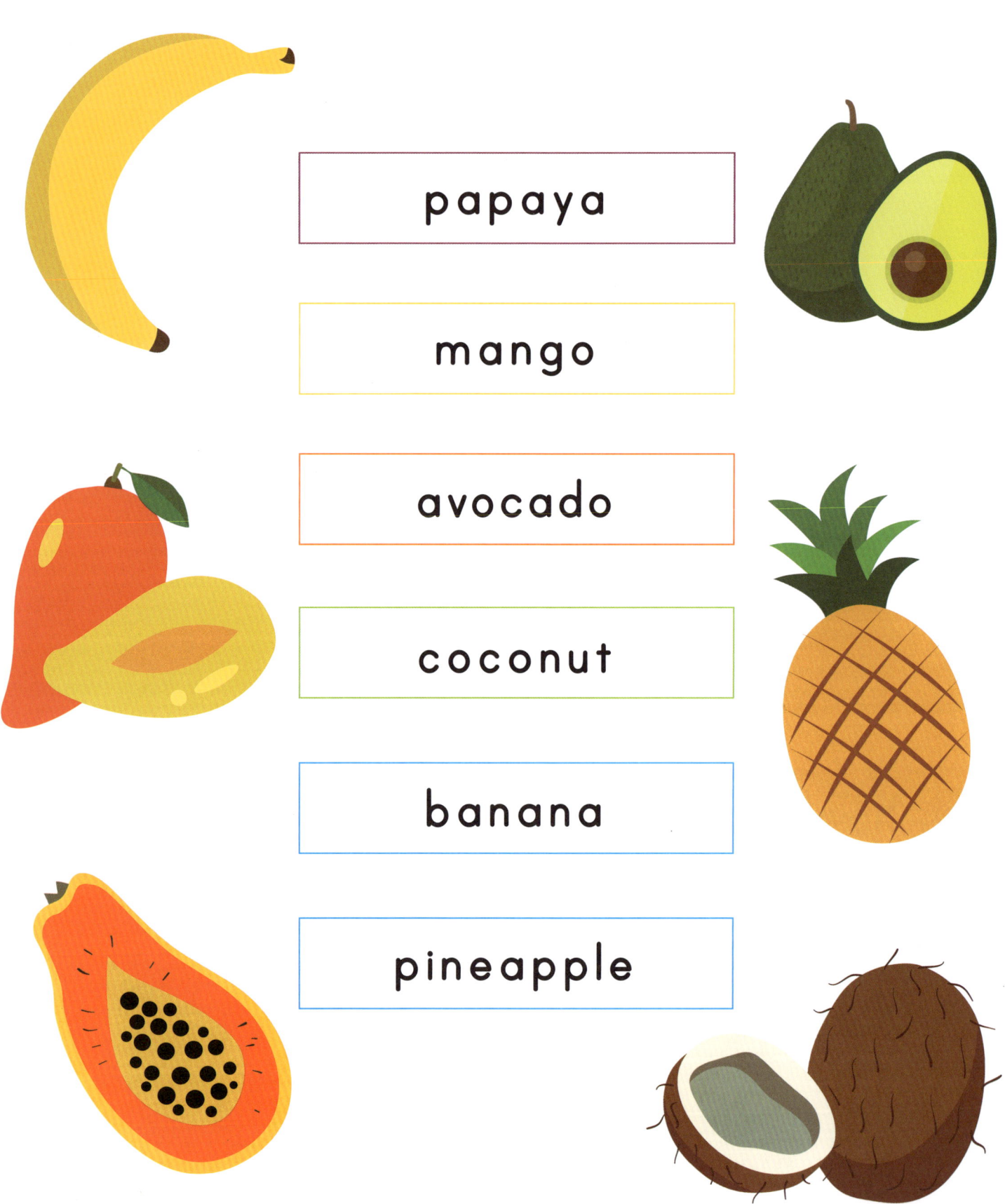

papaya

mango

avocado

coconut

banana

pineapple

Write the name of each fruit under its image.

strawberry • orange • pineapple • banana

Circle the foods you like to eat for breakfast.

Write the word of each object under its image.

bus • notebook • chair • table

Write the correct step numbers for baking cookies:

Steps, 1, 2 and 3:

Steps 4, 5 and 6:

Trace the house and color it in like the example.

In each row, circle the one thing that is different from the others.

Write the correct number next to each action taking place in the image.

1. to draw	4. to slide
2. to swing	5. to climb
3. to paint	6. to hang

Draw a line from each child to the name of the instrument they are playing.

tambourine

maracas

drum

guitar

triangle

violin

Practice writing the word SUMMER.

Summer

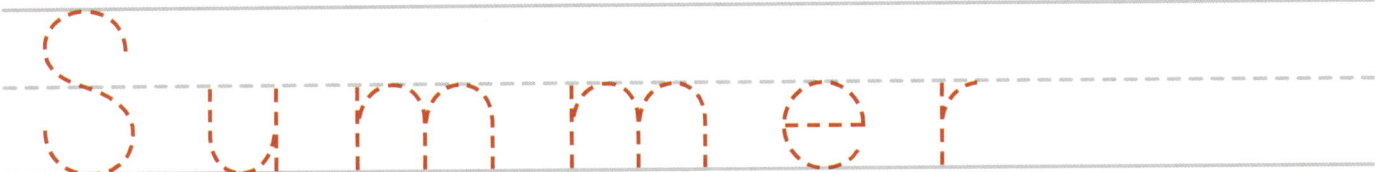

Trace the dotted lines and color in the rainbow.

Practice writing the word RAINBOW.

Rainbow

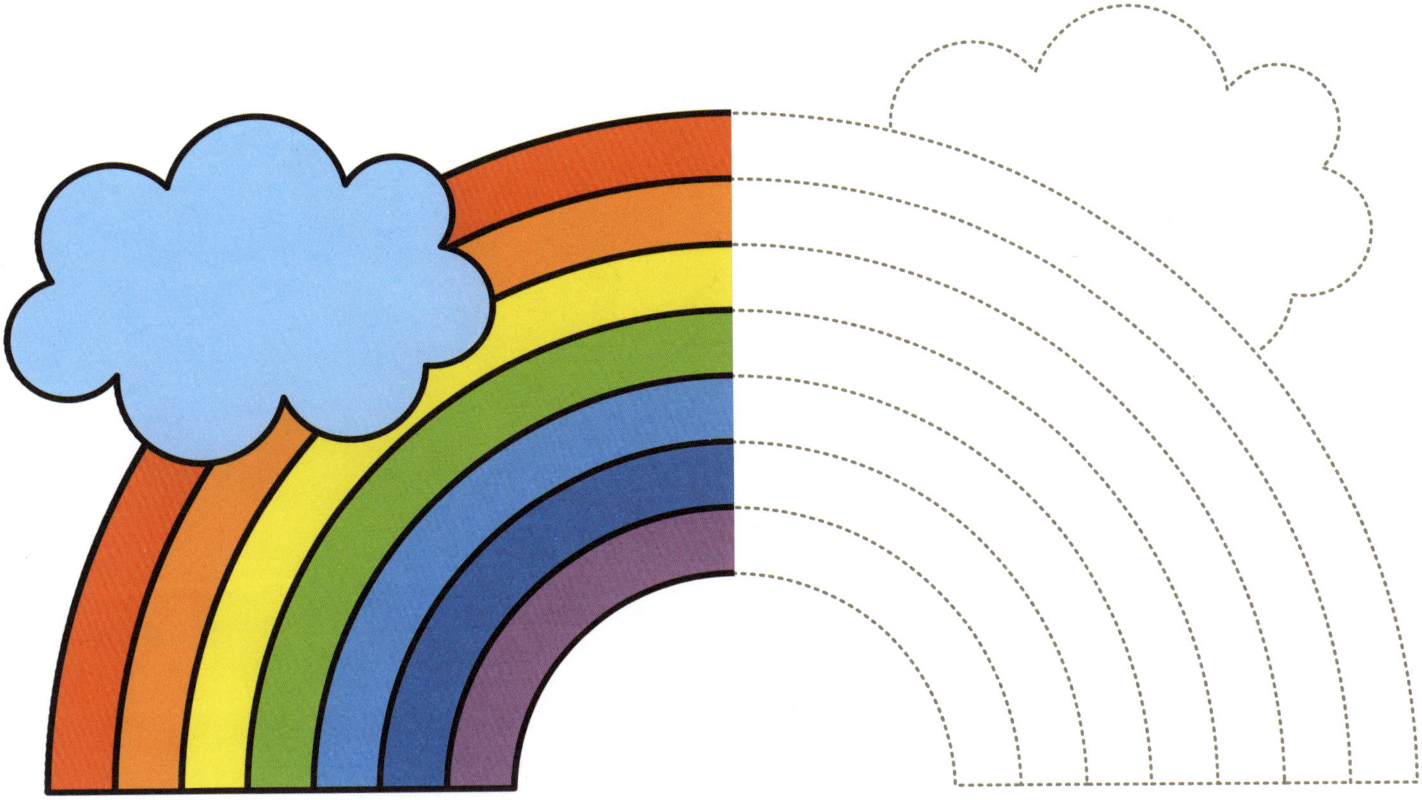

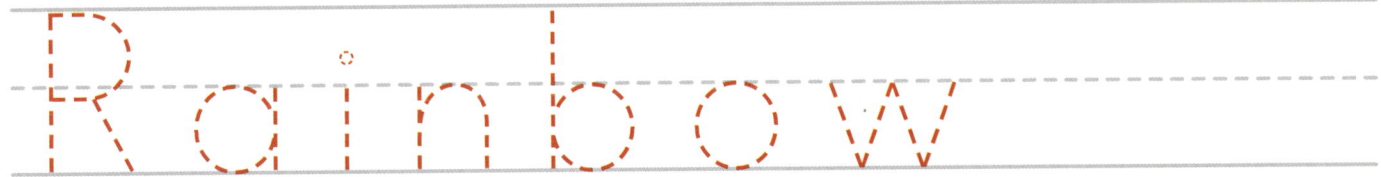

Practice writing the word FALL.

Fall

Trace and color the leaves.

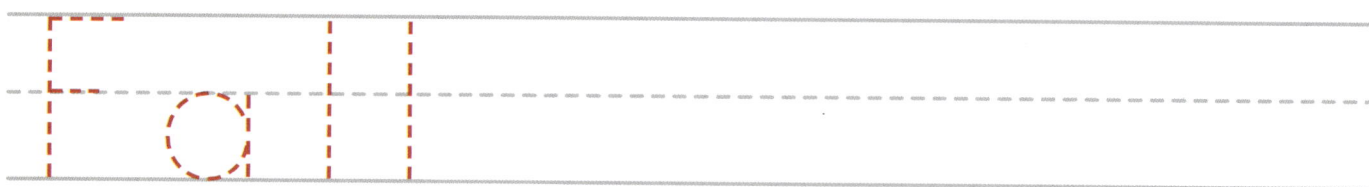

Count all the snowmen that are the same and write how many there are in the circles.

Practice writing the word SPRING.

Spring

Circle the umbrellas that contain all of these colors: 🟢 🔴 🔵

Each shelf is missing a piece. Find the correct piece below and write the letter below each piece in the circle where it belongs.

A   B   C   D   E   F

Find the 12 differences between the two pictures.

Now that you know your alphabet, find a word beginning with each letter and write it on the line.

A _____   N _____

B _____   O _____

C _____   P _____

D _____   Q _____

E _____   R _____

F _____   S _____

G _____   T _____

H _____   U _____

I _____   V _____

J _____   W _____

K _____   X _____

L _____   Y _____

M _____   Z _____

Follow the sequence to go through the maze.